Prudence Hatchett

The Leadership Resilience Workbook

ISBN: 978-1-969463-67-9

Table of Contents

Introduction

This workbook was created for the leaders who are ready to rediscover strength through clarity, compassion, and grounded confidence. It's for the visionary who still believes in purpose but wants to lead without losing themselves in the process.

I've spent over two decades studying human behavior, emotional intelligence, and resilience. What I've learned is simple yet profound, resilience isn't built in moments of crisis; it's built in the moments of practice. Every reflection, every pause, every courageous choice to slow down and reset rewires your brain for endurance, adaptability, and calmness.

Inside, you'll find reflection prompts, self-care templates, leadership case studies, and real-world exercises designed to help you:

- Strengthen your emotional endurance and focus under pressure.
- Build habits that sustain your energy and clarity.
- Transform burnout into balance and overthinking into confident action.
- Reconnect with your purpose, values, and authentic leadership presence.

You'll be challenged to reflect deeply, to identify your patterns, and to rewrite the stories that keep you operating from exhaustion instead of empowerment. You'll learn how resilience becomes the bridge between high performance and emotional wellness between surviving leadership and truly thriving in it.

As you move through each part of this workbook, I invite you to treat these pages like a personal journey for your growth. Write freely. Think critically. Reflect honestly. And most importantly, give yourself permission to rest, reset, and rebuild.

Because great leadership isn't about how much you endure — it's about how well you evolve.

Welcome to The Leadership Resilience Workbook.
Welcome to your reset, your reflection, and your rise.

— Prudence Hatchett
Leadership Resilience Strategist | Board-Certified Coach | Author

Welcome Letter from the Author

I Make Resilience a Lifestyle

Resilience is not just about bouncing back after life or leadership knocks you down, it's about learning to stand taller, think clearer, and lead bolder because of the challenges you've faced. In leadership, resilience is the steady strength that keeps you grounded when pressures rise, the clarity that cuts through chaos, and the courage that turns setbacks into stepping stones.

For me, resilience isn't about perfection, toughness, or ignoring your pain. It's about presence. It's about acknowledging the storm without letting it dictate your direction. It's about training your mind to stay clear when emotions run high, cultivating discipline when distractions pull you sideways, and leaning into courage when fear whispers that you're not enough.

Resilience is the ability to adapt, evolve, and expand without losing your authenticity or your vision. It's the discipline of returning to your "why" when the "how" gets hard. It's the mindset that reminds leaders, you are allowed to bend, but you will not break.

Most importantly, resilience is not a one-time achievement. It's a lifestyle, a daily practice that grows every time you choose clarity over chaos, confidence over fear, and purpose over pressure.

How to Use This Workbook

This workbook is designed as a guide, a mirror, and a practice ground for your leadership resilience. Each section builds on the last, moving you from self-awareness to action, from reflection to bold vision.

Here's how to get the most out of it:

1. Take Your Time
    Don't try to complete the workbook in one sitting. Resilience is built through reflection and repetition. You may return to the same exercises more than once and find your answers change as you grow.

2. Be Honest With Yourself
    These pages are for you, not your board, not your team, not your peers. The deeper your honesty, the greater your breakthrough. Write what you truly feel and think, not what you believe you "should" say.

3. Engage With the Prompts Fully
    Each prompt, activity, and reflection has embedded space for your thoughts. Use it. Don't skip over the questions that make you uncomfortable, those are often where the most growth is waiting.

4. Practice, Don't Just Reflect
    Many sections include activities and behavior swaps. Apply them in real time. Leadership resilience is a skill built through action, not just insight.

5. Revisit and Reassess
    Use the workbook as a leadership companion, not a one-time exercise. Circle back every quarter, every year, or whenever you feel tested. You'll see how far you've come and where you still want to grow.

6. Treat This as Your Leadership Journal
    Capture notes, breakthroughs, quotes, and even your frustrations here. Over time, this workbook becomes your personal record of resilience in motion.

The Leadership Resilience Screener

Instructions: Rate yourself on a scale of 1 (Strongly Disagree) to 5 (Strongly Agree). Provide the answer underneath each statement.

Disclaimer: This screener is for self-reflection only, not for the purpose of providing a diagnosis.

1. I have a clearly defined vision for my team or organization.

____

2. I regularly communicate this vision in a way that inspires others.

____

3. I align my decisions with long-term goals.

____

4. I can make decisions quickly under pressure.

____

5. I avoid letting stress negatively affect my communication.

____

6. I maintain focus on priorities even when overwhelmed.

____

7. I gather enough information before making key decisions.

____

8. I weigh both risks and opportunities effectively.

____

9. I trust my instincts while also valuing data.

10. I am aware of my emotional triggers.

11. I regulate my emotions before responding.

12. I can empathize with others' perspectives.

13. I remain positive during times of change.

14. I help my team adapt to new challenges.

15. I communicate clearly during transitions.

16. I foster a sense of trust in my team.

17. I encourage open and honest communication.

18. I support psychological safety in my workplace.

19. I encourage experimentation within safe boundaries.

20. I see failure as a step toward innovation.

21. I take calculated risks in leadership.

____

22. I stay composed in times of crisis.

____

Self-reported result chart:

- **High scores** (4–5): Strength areas — leverage these in times of uncertainty.
- **Moderate scores** (2–3): Development areas — these are priority growth opportunities.
- **Low scores** (1): Potential blind spots — explore these in coaching to strengthen your leadership foundation.

Is your result surprising or what you expected? Explain your answer.

Self-Awareness & Groundwork

Resilience starts with knowing yourself. In this section, you'll explore how you define resilience, what strengthens you, and identifying your blind spots.

Prompt 1: My definition of resilience is...

Think of resilience not as bouncing back, but as evolving forward. Write your personal definition of resilience in the space below.

____

____

____

____

____

____

____

____

____

____

____

____

____

Prompt 2: When I face challenges, I usually respond by...

This prompt helps you reflect on your default patterns. Do you withdraw, push harder, seek help, or avoid it? Awareness is the first step toward change.

____

____

____

____

____

____

____

____

____

____

____

____

____

Think of a moment where you endure pressure or setback. What did you learn about yourself? How did it shape your leadership?

____

____

____

____

____

____

____

____

____

____

____

____

____

____

Leadership Pain Points

Even the strongest leaders have pain points. Understanding these areas helps you create strategies for resilience instead of being blindsided by challenges.

Prompt 1: I tend to lose clarity when...

Notice what situations cause confusion, overwhelm, or indecision. Awareness builds resilience.

Prompt 2: The biggest energy drains in my leadership are...

Energy drains can come from people, processes, or even personal habits.

____

____

____

____

____

____

____

____

____

____

____

____

____

Prompt 3: I know I am slipping into burnout when...

List the early warning signs, physical, emotional, or behavioral
that tell you resilience is fading.

____

____

____

____

____

____

____

____

____

____

____

____

____

____

Write honestly about truths you've ignored or minimized. These hidden pain points often block resilience.

____

____

____

____

____

____

____

____

____

____

____

____

____

____

Emotional Regulation & Mindset

Emotional regulation is not about avoiding emotions; it's about learning how to control them. Leaders who regulate their emotions maintain clarity even in chaos.

Prompt 1: When I feel stress in my body, I notice it in...

Stress shows up physically (i.e. shoulders, chest, feet). Write about where you notice the most stress and when.

____

____

____

____

____

____

____

____

____

____

____

____

____

____

Prompt 2: List 10 emotions I usually avoid in leadership.

Naming emotions helps you expand emotional range and resilience (tip: use Google to research different emotions).

____

____

____

____

____

____

____

____

____

____

____

____

____

____

____

Activity: Nervous System Reset Tracker

Create a list of strategies that calm your nervous system
(breathing, grounding, stretching) and make note of how you feel
before and after use.

____

____

____

____

____

____

____

____

____

____

____

____

____

Stress & Resilience

Resilient leaders make themselves aware of their stressors to create clarity in making decisions.

Prompt 1: Top 5 stressors in my role are...

Writing them, clearly naming them, reduces their power.

Prompt 2: I can improve resilience by letting go of... and holding onto...

Identify habits to release, and strengths to hold on to.

____

____

____

____

____

____

____

____

____

____

____

____

____

____

Activity: Stress Audit

Track when and where stress shows up in your week. Note triggers and patterns.

____

____

____

____

____

____

____

____

____

____

____

____

____

____

____

____

Resilient Behaviors in Action

Leadership resilience is measured in behaviors. Shifting from reactive to resilient actions changes the tone of leadership.

Prompt 1: Instead of micromanaging when anxious, I will...

Micromanagement can signal fear and distrust.

Avoidance prolongs stress.

Prompt 3: Resilient behaviors I want to model are...

Think of how you want your team to describe your leadership under stress.

____

____

____

____

____

____

____

____

____

____

____

____

____

____

Building Your Leadership System

Resilience doesn't exist in isolation. Strong leaders cultivate systems that sustain clarity, confidence, and connection.

Think about how your actions build or drain resilience in your team.

Prompt 2: What team culture am I building?

Your default responses often set the tone for team culture.

Future-Focused Growth

Resilient leaders are future builders. They look beyond setbacks and shape bold visions.

Prompt 1: The bold leader I am becoming is...

Write a vision statement for the leader you want to grow into.

____

____

____

____

____

____

____

____

____

____

____

____

____

____

____

Prompt 2: In 1 year, my resilience will look like...

Describe your growth goals for the next year.

Prompt 3: One bold vision I am ready to claim is...

Write the vision that excites and challenges you the most.

____

____

____

____

____

____

____

____

____

____

____

____

____

____

____

Values Under Pressure

List your top 5 values. Then reflect on how you uphold them when under stress or facing tough decisions.

Activity: Future Self Letter

Write a letter to yourself one year from now, celebrating your resilience and growth.

____

____

____

____

____

____

____

____

____

____

____

____

____

____

Resilience rituals I can create daily are...

Small rituals can regulate your nervous system: deep breathing, journaling, mindful walks. Create your list.

____

____

____

____

____

____

____

____

____

____

____

____

____

____

Crisis Leadership Simulations

Instructions: Read each scenario carefully. Write your immediate response strategy and longer-term resilience approach. Use these to rehearse crisis thinking in advance.

Financial Shock

Your organization faces an unexpected 30% revenue drop due to market changes.

How do you respond in the first 48 hours, and what is your long-term recovery plan?

____

____

____

____

____

____

____

____

____

____

____

____

____

Public Reputation Crisis

A negative news story about your company is going viral. Employees are anxious and stakeholders demand answers. How do you communicate and act under scrutiny?

____

____

____

____

____

____

____

____

____

____

____

____

____

____

Team Burnout

Your top-performing team shows signs of burnout during a critical project deadline. What steps do you take to balance delivery and well-being?

A major system outage halts core business operation for 24 hours. How do you manage the crisis internally and externally?

Leadership Transition

You must suddenly take over a division after another leader's abrupt exit. How do you stabilize the team and establish trust quickly?

____

____

____

____

____

____

____

____

____

____

____

Leadership Transition

____

Shadow Self & Leadership

The *shadow self* is the part of us that holds the traits, emotions, and desires we often suppress, deny, or dislike. It's not inherently "bad"—it's simply the hidden side of our personality that stays out of sight because it feels uncomfortable to acknowledge. This can include unexpressed anger, ambition, fear, envy, or even creative impulses we've been taught to downplay. By ignoring the shadow, we risk letting it unconsciously influence our behaviors in ways we don't recognize.

In leadership, the shadow self can intertwine with how we lead teams, make decisions, and handle power. A leader who hasn't faced their shadow may project insecurity as control, turn fear into micromanagement, or suppress creativity in others because it mirrors something they haven't embraced in themselves. On the other hand, when leaders engage with their shadow, they develop greater self-awareness, empathy, and authenticity. This integration helps them model resilience, navigate conflict with clarity, and create environments where others feel safe to be whole and authentic too.

Here are five critical-thinking self-reflection questions. These questions will help unblock blind spots or hidden areas that need your attention for improving leadership resilience.

Note: Think of a real-life leadership challenge you experienced.

What patterns do I notice in my reactions to challenges, and what these patterns might reveal about my beliefs or fears?

____

____

____

____

____

____

____

____

____

____

____

____

____

____

Am I making decisions based on evidence and values, or on assumptions and emotions I haven't examined? Describe the scenarios based on the latter.

____

____

____

____

____

____

____

____

____

____

____

____

____

____

____

How might someone with a completely different perspective view one of my toughest challenges, and what could I learn from that angle?

What part of me feels uncomfortable or defensive, and what might that discomfort be trying to teach me?

If I step back and look at the long-term impact of my choices, how would these choices shape the leader, partner, or person I want to become?

Shadow Work Reflection Exercises:

Spotting Bias & Blind Spots

- **Prompt:** Think of a recent leadership decision you made. Who benefited most from it? Who might have been overlooked?
- **Exercise:** Write down two assumptions you made at that moment. Then ask yourself: *What evidence did I have? What evidence did I ignore?*
- **Reflection Goal:** Increase awareness of unconscious influences on your leadership.

Leadership Under Pressure

- **Prompt:** Recall a high-stress moment with your team. How did you respond—did you lean toward control, withdrawal, or collaboration?
- **Exercise:** Journal about what you *needed* in that moment (e.g., clarity, certainty, validation). Then ask: *How could I have met that need while still empowering my team?*
- **Reflection Goal:** Strengthen resilience and shift from reactive to intentional leadership.

Facing Resistance to Feedback

- **Prompt:** Write down one piece of feedback you've received that still stings or feels unfair.
- **Exercise:** Divide a page into two columns: on the left, write your immediate defensive reaction. On the right, write what truth or lesson *might* exist beneath it.
- **Reflection Goal:** Transform defensiveness into growth by reframing feedback as insight.

Aligning Words & Actions

- **Prompt:** List your top three leadership values (e.g., integrity, innovation, compassion).
- **Exercise:** For each value, write one example of when you lived it fully, and one example where your actions fell short. What created the gap?
- **Reflection Goal:** Build consistency between what you say and what you model.

Leading with Trust vs. Control

- **Prompt:** Reflect on a recent time you delegated a task. Did you truly let go, or did you keep control through check-ins or corrections?
- **Exercise:** Write down what "trusting your team" looks like in action. Then, set one small experiment this week to practice releasing control in a safe area.
- **Reflection Goal:** Develop a culture of empowerment and trust.

Fill-in-the-blank Reflections

Here's a set of 20 fill-in-the-blank reflection questions to use for honest self-reflection. They're open-ended so you can personalize the answers.

Self-Awareness

1. The leadership quality I most want to strengthen is __________

2. When I feel overwhelmed, my default reaction is __________

3. The belief I hold about myself that helps me lead with confidence is __________

4. A blind spot I suspect I might have is __________

Values & Purpose

1. The value I never want to compromise as a leader is __________

2. My leadership is at its best when I am guided by __________

3. I feel most fulfilled in my role when I am __________

4. The purpose of my leadership is to __________

Relationships & Influence

1. The way I want people to feel after working with me is __________

2. When others give me feedback, I usually respond by
   ____

3. The type of support I most need from my team is
   ____

4. A conversation I've been avoiding but need to have is with
   ____

Growth & Resilience

1. The last time I stepped outside my comfort zone as a
   leader, I ___________

2. The most important lesson I've learned from a failure is
   ____

3. I know I'm growing as a leader when I notice ___________

4. The resilience practice that helps me recover from
   setbacks is ___________

Vision & Impact

1. If my leadership had a headline today, it would read
   ____

2. The legacy I want to leave as a leader is ___________

3. The impact I most want to have on my team or
   organization is ___________

4. A bold step I need to take in the next year is ___________

Find the Leadership Mistake

Read each story and identify the leadership mistakes. Write down all that you can find, then write down what that leader can do instead.

#1

For the past three weeks, the team has been staying late into the night to hit an aggressive product launch deadline. Some employees have started making mistakes from exhaustion, while others quietly express frustration. In a staff meeting, one team member cautiously mentions that people are burning out and struggling to keep pace. The leader, already stressed, shrugs it off and reminds them that "this is just part of the job" before pushing everyone to double down even harder.

#2

Two high performers on the same project begin clashing over ownership and direction. Their tension has grown so obvious that meetings are awkward, and tasks are falling behind. Instead of addressing the conflict, the leader pretends not to notice. Weeks go by, the tension escalates, and productivity drops further. The leader continues to assign work without acknowledging the elephant in the room.

#3

During a one-on-one, a team member nervously brings up that the leader's tone in group meetings sometimes feels harsh and dismissive. The employee explains that it makes them hesitant to share ideas. The leader immediately bristles, insists that they're just being "direct," and tells the employee to "toughen up" if they want to succeed in this environment.

____

____

____

____

____

____

____

____

____

____

____

____

____

#4

In a brainstorming session, a junior employee offers a bold new idea that challenges the standard way of doing things. The room falls silent, waiting to see how the leader will respond. The leader frowns and quickly shuts down the suggestion, saying it's "not how we do things here." The discussion moves on, and the employee who spoke up quietly withdraws for the rest of the meeting.

____

____

____

____

____

____

____

____

____

____

____

____

#5

A key project hits a delay, and senior executives demand an update. The leader storms into the room, red-faced, and berates the team for "dropping the ball." Team members try to explain the external factors that caused the delay, but the leader continues venting frustration, pointing fingers, and leaving the group feeling deflated and fearful.

6

With pressure mounting, the leader becomes increasingly anxious about the team's performance. They start hovering over each detail of the project, rewriting emails, redoing presentations, and questioning every small step. Instead of empowering the team, the leader takes control of tasks themselves, leaving employees disengaged and second-guessing their own abilities.

#7

During a strategy session, a team member expresses feeling left out of decision-making and raises concerns about inclusivity in the group. Instead of engaging with the issue, the leader brushes it off, saying, "We're all the same here—there's no need to bring that up." The employee falls silent, while others glance around the room uncertainly, sensing that the concern has been dismissed.

____

____

____

____

____

____

____

____

____

____

____

____

#8

A major decision about allocating budget resources is due, but the leader feels uncertain about which direction to take. Rather than gathering input or making a timely choice, they repeatedly delay the conversation. The team, unsure of the priorities, stalls in their work, frustrated that no clear direction has been given. Weeks later, the decision remains unresolved, and opportunities have been missed.

____

____

____

____

____

____

____

____

____

____

____

____

#9

After a disappointing product launch, executives demand accountability. In a tense meeting, the leader points to another department as the source of the failure, insisting that it wasn't their responsibility. The team listens silently, frustrated that their leader has distanced themselves from the outcome instead of addressing the deeper issues that led to the poor result.

#10

The CEO asks the leader if the team can meet an almost impossible deadline for a high-profile project. Without hesitation, the leader agrees, assuring the CEO it will get done. Later, the leader returns to the team and announces the deadline, knowing it will require long nights, weekends, and likely burnout. The team looks defeated before even starting, aware that failure or exhaustion is inevitable.

Leadership Resilience Affirmations

Write each affirmation 5 times.

"I lead with calm strength, even when the storm is loud."

____

____

____

____

____

"Every challenge sharpens my clarity, focus, and resolve."

____

____

____

____

____

"I adapt quickly, without losing sight of my values."

____

____

____

____

*"My resilience is not about being unshakable,
it's about always rising."*

____

____

____

____

"I transform obstacles into opportunities for growth and innovation."

____

____

____

____

____

5 Ways Leaders Self–Sabotage

Leadership isn't about flawless execution, it's about resilience, adaptability, and growth. Yet even the most seasoned leaders can unknowingly fall into patterns of self-sabotage. These patterns don't just harm them, they ripple out, affecting teams, culture, and results. Below are five common traps for leaders. The next page includes how to break free from these traps. You will match the correct answer to the trap.

Micromanagement often comes from fear—fear that mistakes will reflect poorly on the leader or that letting go means losing control. While the intention may be to ensure quality, the outcome is the opposite. Teams under a micromanager feel suffocated, disengaged, and uninspired to bring forward new ideas.

____

Leaders who sidestep conflict may think they're protecting harmony, but in reality, silence creates bigger problems. Unaddressed issues breed resentment, miscommunication, and team dysfunction. Avoidance erodes credibility because people notice when leaders refuse to confront what matters.

____

Many leaders pride themselves on being the hardest workers in the room, but this often backfires. When leaders run on empty, they lose clarity, patience, and creativity the very qualities their teams need most. Burnout at the top trickles down and becomes burnout for everyone.

____

Perfectionism masquerades as high standards, but in reality, it slows progress and creates fear. Leaders stuck in "it's not good enough" mode stall projects, exhaust their teams, and miss opportunities to learn through action.

____

Leaders often dedicate energy to developing their teams but neglect their own development. Over time, this creates blind spots, outdated thinking, and resistance to change. When leaders stop learning, organizations stop evolving.

____

Answers:

A. Stay in student mode. Read widely, seek mentors, welcome feedback, and invest in training or coaching. The best leaders model growth by showing they, too, are willing to evolve.

B. Move from control to clarity. Set clear expectations, share the "why" behind the work, and then step back. Trust builds engagement, and engagement builds results.

C. Trade perfection for progress. Encourage experimentation, celebrate learning from mistakes, and model flexibility. Excellence comes from iteration, not unattainable flawlessness.

D. Reframe tough conversations as opportunities for alignment and growth. Approach them with curiosity rather than judgment, and focus on outcomes, not blame.

E. Treat self-care as a leadership responsibility, not a luxury. Rest, reflection, and boundaries make leaders sharper and more effective. A healthy leader sets the tone for a healthy team.

Leadership Activities

1. Resilience Timeline

Draw a timeline of your leadership journey. Mark 3–5 significant challenges you faced. For each, write how you reacted at the time and what you would do differently today with stronger resilience.

____

____

____

____

____

____

____

____

____

____

____

____

____

____

2. Values in Action

List your top 5 personal values. Then, write an example of how each value has shaped a leadership decision in the past. Circle one value you want to practice more intentionally at work.

____

____

____

____

____

____

____

____

____

____

____

____

____

3. Energy Audit

Divide a page into two columns: "Energizers" and "Drainers." Fill in what tasks, people, or environments fuel your energy vs. deplete it. Reflect: *How can I restructure my week to increase energizers and manage drainers?*

____

____

____

____

____

____

____

____

____

____

____

____

____

4. The Mirror Test

Write a paragraph answering: "If my team were asked to describe my leadership style in one sentence today, what would they say?" Then, write the sentence you want them to say. Compare the two and identify the gap.

5. Case Study Reframe

Choose a leadership scenario experienced by someone else (i.e. peer, colleague, tv show). Describe how the leader reacted. Then rewrite the story showing a resilient, confident, emotionally regulated response.

____

____

____

____

____

____

____

____

____

____

____

____

____

____

6. The 5 Whys

Your team lacks motivation, why?

Your sleeping habits are getting worse everyday, why?

A team member unexpectedly quit, why?

After a meeting with the CEO, you wanted to quit, why?

You think you deserve a raise, why?

____

____

____

____

____

____

____

____

____

____

____

____

7. Resilient Alternatives

List 5 unhelpful leadership habits you've noticed in yourself (e.g., overcommitting, micromanaging, delaying decisions). Next to each one, write a "resilient alternative" that would produce better outcomes.

____

____

____

____

____

____

____

____

____

____

____

____

____

8. Vision Journal

Imagine it's 3 years from now and you've mastered resilient leadership. Write a one-page journal entry as if you're living in that future. Describe your impact, team culture, and how you feel in your role.

____

____

____

____

____

____

____

____

____

____

____

____

____

9. Resilience Rituals Map

List your current activities/behaviors in your daily routine. Circle which ones build resilience (e.g., journaling, exercise, mindful breaks), and draw a line through the ones that don't (e.g. oversleeping, skipping lunch). Add 2 new activities/behaviors you want to implement to strengthen mental clarity and confidence.

____

____

____

____

____

____

____

____

____

____

____

____

10. Feedback Flip

Recall a piece of feedback that stung. Write down the feedback,
your initial emotional reaction, and how you responded. Then
rewrite how a resilient leader would interpret and use that
feedback as fuel for growth.

11. Leaders Don't Whine

I made a post on social media that stated, "Leaders don't whine, they get to work." I want you to write 10 taglines using "Leaders don't whine,______________"

12. Leadership Brag Time

This is not the time to be bashful, this is the time to be bold. Write 10 leadership brag statements. Make them personal.

____

____

____

____

____

____

____

____

____

____

____

____

____

____

____

13. The Stress Snapshot

Draw a circle and divide it into sections labeled: Workload, Relationships, Decision-Making, Self-Doubt, and External Pressures. Shade each slice to represent how much stress it currently causes you.

____

____

____

____

____

____

____

____

____

____

____

____

____

14. Leadership Compass

Draw a compass with four points: North = Vision, East = People, South = Strategy, West = Self. Write one strength and one growth area in each direction. Ask: Which point am I neglecting most?

____

____

____

____

____

____

____

____

____

____

____

____

____

15. Courage Inventory

Make a list of 5 situations you've avoided recently because of fear, uncertainty, or discomfort. Next to each one, write a courageous first step you could take this week.

____

____

____

____

____

____

____

____

____

____

____

____

____

16. Impact 360

Write down three words you believe described your leadership in the past, three words that describe your leadership now, and three words that describe your leadership in the future. Compare and Contrast.

____

____

____

____

____

____

____

____

____

____

____

____

17. The Resilient Leader's Playlist

List 5 songs, quotes, or mantras that energize you. Then, write a short reflection on how each connects to your leadership journey. (Example: "This song reminds me that setbacks don't define me.")

____

____

____

____

____

____

____

____

____

____

____

____

____

18. The "What If" Flip

Identify a negative thought you've had about leadership this month (e.g., What if I fail?). Rewrite it as a positive, resilient question (e.g., What if this challenge helps me grow?). Practice flipping 5 thoughts this way.

---

19. Boundary Builder

List the top 3 situations where your boundaries are often crossed
(e.g., after-hours texts, unrealistic deadlines). Write the exact
words you could use to set a firm but professional boundary in
each case.

____

____

____

____

____

____

____

____

____

____

____

____

____

20. Decision Map

Think of a recent decision that felt overwhelming. Map out three possible choices. Circle the one that aligns most with your long-term leadership vision.

____

____

____

____

____

____

____

____

____

____

____

____

____

21. Gratitude List

Write 10 reasons why you're grateful for your leadership journey. Reflect: How does gratitude shift my perspective when things get hard?

22. The Legacy Letter

Write a one-page letter addressed to your future team, 10 years from now. Describe the kind of culture you hope they're thriving in because of your leadership. Ask yourself: What steps can I take today to make this letter true?

____

____

____

____

____

____

____

____

____

____

____

____

____

____

23. Leadership Resilience True or False

1. Conflict within a team is always a negative sign.

2. A leader's emotional tone directly influences team performance.

3. Delegating tasks means giving up control and risking failure.

4. Leaders who admit mistakes lose credibility.

5. Resilience is built only through overcoming major crises.

6. Setting clear boundaries makes leaders more respected, not less.

7. Burnout only affects employees, not leaders.

8. Effective feedback requires both honesty and empathy.

9. Vision without consistent action is just an idea.

10. Strong leaders should always have the answers.

5 Core Leadership Challenges

1. Navigating Uncertainty

Leadership often requires making decisions with incomplete information. The pressure to appear confident while doubts swirl internally can feel overwhelming. Resilient leaders don't ignore the uncertainty; they lean into it with strategic questioning, and the courage to decide anyway.

Reflection Prompts:

- What is the biggest uncertain situation I'm currently facing?

- How do I typically respond when I don't have all the answers?

- What practices help me stay grounded when outcomes are unclear?

2. Managing Conflict Effectively

Conflict is not always a sign of failure, it can be a sign that people care enough to have strong opinions. Avoiding it erodes trust, while mishandling it damages relationships. The resilient leader listens actively, addresses issues directly, and creates pathways for resolution.

Reflection Prompts:

- How do I usually react when tension arises on my team?

- What recent conflict did I avoid or escalate unnecessarily?

- What tools or language could I use to turn conflict into collaboration?

3. Balancing Compassion and Accountability

It can be difficult to be both empathetic and firm. Leaders sometimes swing too far either being overly lenient or excessively demanding. The resilient leader sets high standards while also supporting their team through challenges, showing that care and accountability are not opposites.

Reflection Prompts:

- Do I tend to over-emphasize compassion or accountability?

- How do I know when my team feels both supported and challenged?

- What boundary or expectation do I need to clarify right now?

4. Sustaining Energy and Avoiding Burnout

Leadership is a marathon, not a sprint. Yet many leaders deplete themselves trying to "push through." Resilient leaders model sustainable habits such as rest, reflection, and renewal because they know their energy sets the tone for the entire organization.

Reflection Prompts:

- Where do I notice the first signs of burnout in myself?

- What rituals keep my energy strong and my clarity sharp?

- How can I better model healthy boundaries for my team?

5. Maintaining Vision Under Pressure

When challenges mount, leaders often get trapped in reactive mode. The resilient leader holds on to the bigger picture, reminding themselves and their teams of the "why" behind the work. Vision is the anchor that steadies the ship during storms.

Reflection Prompts:

- When I feel pressure, do I lose sight of the long-term vision?

- How do I communicate vision in a way that inspires others during difficulty?

- What one bold step can I take this month to realign with my vision?

Resilience Coping Strategy Toolkit

Deep Breathing:

Inhale deeply through the nose for 4 counts, hold for 4, exhale slowly through the mouth for 6–8 counts. Repeat 3–5 times.

Meditation

Start with 5 minutes daily. Focus on your breath, a single word (like clarity), soft music, or a calming image.

Stress Management Tips

- Identify triggers and label them.
- Break large problems into smaller, actionable steps.
- Schedule recovery time such as short walks, listening to music, or intentional breaks.

Relaxation Practices

- Progressive muscle relaxation: tense each muscle group for 5 seconds, then release.
- Grounding: place both feet flat, notice 3 things you see, 2 things you hear, 1 thing you feel.
- Use guided relaxation apps for 10-minute resets.

Reframing

- Shift from "Why is this happening to me?" to "What is this teaching me?"
- Ask yourself: "Is there another perspective that creates opportunity here?"

Countering Negative Thoughts

- Write the negative thoughts down.
- Challenge it with facts: "Is this 100% true?"
- Replace with a balanced truth: "This is hard, but I have the skills to handle it."

Communication

- Be clear, concise, and consistent.
- Use active listening: repeat back what you hear to confirm understanding.
- Match tone with message, calm tone builds trust, even in conflict.

Prioritizing

- Use the 80/20 rule: focus on the 20% of tasks that drive 80% of results.
- Ask daily: "What is most important right now?"
- Protect time for high-value tasks first, not last.

Time Management

- Pre-plan your day. Waiting to the day-of to plan can increase stress
- Use the 2-minute rule: if it takes less than 2 minutes, do it now.
- Review your calendar weekly: remove what doesn't align with your goals or no longer necessary.

Organization

- Start with one system: digital planner, task manager, or physical notebook.
- Keep a running list for ideas that distract you during focus work.
- Declutter weekly, physical space impacts mental clarity.

Energy Management

- Track energy, not just time, notice when you're sharpest and schedule demanding tasks there.
- Build in recovery rituals: hydration, stretching, walking calls.
- Protect sleep as a leadership tool, not a luxury.

30 Day Leadership Resilience Self-care Plan

Use this plan as a guide, feel free to "plug-in" any of the strategies that fit you best.

Reminder: Make resilience a lifestyle.

Day 1: Reset & Reflect

Morning: 10 minutes of deep breathing or mindfulness.
Midday: Write down the top 3 values guiding your leadership this week.
Evening Reflection: What areas were I challenged the most?

Day 2: Physical Energy Check

Morning: Light movement or stretching.
Midday: Choose nourishing food.
Evening Reflection: How did my energy level impact my leadership today?

Day 3: Emotional Awareness

Morning: Journal one positive affirmation about your leadership resilience.
Midday: Pause before a meeting, name your current emotion.
Evening Reflection: When did I regulate my emotions well today? When did I struggle?

Day 4: Connection & Support

Morning: Send one note of gratitude or encouragement to a team member.
Midday: Schedule a 5-minute check-in with a peer, mentor, or coach.
Evening Reflection: Did I ask for help today, or try to carry everything myself?

Day 5: Vision Alignment

Morning: Read or recite your personal leadership vision statement.
Midday: Review this week's decisions, did they align with your bigger vision?
Evening Reflection: Where did I get reactive today, and how could I have stayed anchored in vision?

Day 6: Boundaries & Renewal

Morning: Write one boundary you will honor today (e.g., no emails after 7pm).
Midday: Take a short break outdoors or away from screens.
Evening Reflection: What boundary did I keep that protected my energy?

Day 7: Gratitude & Growth

Morning: List 5 things you're grateful for in your leadership journey.

Midday: Identify 1 area of growth you want to carry into the next week.

Evening Reflection: How did self-care shape my resilience this week?

Day 8: Mental Clarity

Morning: 5 minutes of silence before turning on devices.
Midday: Write your top 3 priorities for today.
Evening Reflection: Did I protect my mental space today?

Day 9: Courage in Leadership

Morning: Affirm one bold decision you will make this week.
Midday: Take one small action on something you've delayed.
Evening Reflection: What did I do today that required courage?

Day 10: Mind-Body Reset

Morning: Stretch or walk for 10 minutes.
Midday: Drink water instead of caffeine at least once.
Evening Reflection: How did movement shift my energy?

Day 11: Listening Practice

Morning: Intend to listen more than you speak in one meeting.
Midday: Ask one open-ended question to a team member.
Evening Reflection: What did I hear today that I might have missed before?

Day 12: Self-Compassion

Morning: Write one kind sentence to yourself about your leadership.
Midday: Pause and notice any harsh self-talk. Replace it with encouragement.
Evening Reflection: Where did I extend compassion to myself today?

Day 13: Renewal Rituals

Morning: Identify one small joy to schedule today (walk, music, laughter).
Midday: Take 5 minutes to do that activity, guilt-free.
Evening Reflection: What lifted my spirit today?

Day 14: Alignment Check

Morning: Revisit your leadership vision statement.
Midday: Compare one decision today against your long-term goals.
Evening Reflection: Where did I lead from alignment today?

Day 15: Stress Awareness

Morning: Rate your stress from 1–10.
Midday: Meditate for 5 minutes.
Evening Reflection: What helped me regulate stress today?

Day 16: Creative Space

Morning: Spend 10 minutes brainstorming a challenge.
Midday: Share one creative idea with a peer.
Evening Reflection: What creativity surfaced when I gave myself space?

Day 17: Feedback Strength

Morning: Intend to ask for feedback from one person today.
Midday: Record what they shared (without defending yourself).
Evening Reflection: What truth did I hear, and how can I use it?

Day 18: Patience Practice

Morning: Breathe before responding to an email or request.
Midday: Notice when you feel rushed and pause for perspective.
Evening Reflection: When did I practice patience today?

Day 19: Energy Reset

Morning: Journal. What drains me? What fuels me?
Midday: Do one activity from your "fuels me" list.
Evening Reflection: How did I protect my energy today?

Day 20: Leadership Presence

Morning: Take 3 deep breaths, and envision how you want to show up today.
Midday: Notice your body language in a meeting. Were you open & confident?

Evening Reflection: How did my presence influence others?

Day 21: Rest & Renewal

Morning: Commit to unplugging for 1 hour today.
Midday: Use that hour for non-work activity (nature, family, silence).
Evening Reflection: How did rest strengthen me as a leader today?

Day 22: Decision Confidence

Morning: Recall a strong decision you've made in the past.
Midday: Make one pending decision with confidence.
Evening Reflection: What did I learn about my decision-making today?

Day 23: Gratitude in Leadership

Morning: Write down 3 team wins from the past week.
Midday: Publicly thank them for their contribution.
Evening Reflection: How did gratitude shift the energy of my team?

Day 24: Emotional Check-In

Morning: Write your emotional state in one word.
Midday: Name and accept emotions during a stressful moment.
Evening Reflection: How did emotional awareness guide my responses?

Day 25: Boundaries with Technology

Morning: Choose a time to turn off devices tonight.
Midday: Notice how often you check your phone.
Evening Reflection: *Did my boundary with tech improve my clarity today?*

Day 26: Resilient Reframing

Morning: Write down one negative thought about leadership.
Midday: Rewrite it into a resilient perspective.
Evening Reflection: What did reframing teach me today?

Day 27: Team Connection

Morning: Intend to notice strengths in others today.
Midday: Share one piece of positive feedback.
Evening Reflection: How did I lift up others today, and how did they respond?

Day 28: Self-Trust

Morning: Journal. What is one small promise I'll keep to myself today?
Midday: Follow through on it.
Evening Reflection: Did I honor my own word?

Day 29: Legacy Focus

Morning: Imagine your team 5 years from now. Write one sentence about the culture you want them to describe.

Midday: Identify one action today that moves toward that legacy.

Evening Reflection: What step did I take toward the leader I want to be remembered as?

Day 30: Celebrate & Commit

Morning: Write down 5 resilience practices you want to carry forward.

Midday: Share one insight with your team, coach, or peer.

Evening Reflection: How has 30 days of resilience practices reshaped me as a leader?

Create Your Own Leadership Resilience Self-care Plan

(Day 1) Day of the week:

Morning:

Midday:

Evening Reflection:

(Day 2) Day of the week:

Morning:

Midday:

Evening Reflection:

(Day 3) Day of the week:

Morning:

Midday:

Evening Reflection:

(Day 4) Day of the week:

Morning:

Midday:

Evening Reflection:

(Day 5) **Day of the week:**

Morning:

Midday:

Evening Reflection:

(Day 6) **Day of the week:**

Morning:

Midday:

Evening Reflection:

(Day 7) **Day of the week:**

Morning:

Midday:

Evening Reflection:

About the Author

Prudence Hatchett is a Leadership Resilience Strategist who helps leaders cultivate bold resilience that fuels inspiration, impact, and sustainable success. She is also the founder of **PH Counseling, LLC™** and the creator of the premium mental wellness brand **Learn with Prudence™**. Prudence is a **3x best-selling solo author** and **5x best-selling co-author**, an accomplished business owner, global speaker, National Certified Counselor, multi-state Licensed Professional Counselor, Board Qualified Clinical Supervisor, Board Certified Coach, multi-endorsed Master Educator, and multi-certified mental health professional. With over 20 years of experience, she brings a unique blend of clinical expertise and real-world leadership insight. Prudence empowers people to strengthen emotional wellness, and step into their highest potential through the power of resilience.

Accelerated Leadership Resilience Program

"A resilience program that empowers your leadership purpose, presence, & influence."

Leadership pain points:

- *Lack of recovery practices* leading to burnout and disengagement.
- *Emotional exhaustion* from constant demands and high-stakes leadership.
- *Decision fatigue* and reduced clarity under pressure.
- *Difficulty managing conflict* with emotional balance.
- *Fear of vulnerability, rejection, or disrespect,* creating disconnection with teams and leadership purpose.

Leadership Power Gains:

- Eliminate burnout and rebuild emotional endurance.
- Increase emotional intelligence and executive decision-making.
- Lead with clarity and confidence under pressure.
- Regain control of your energy, time, and emotional balance.
- Improve decision-making and reduce stress-driven mistakes.
- Model resilience, earning respect and trust from your team.
- ...include personalized goals

Why choose ME as your coach?

With 20+ years of experience as a licensed counselor, board-certified coach, master educator, and bestselling author, I've helped leaders at every level strengthen resilience, elevate their leadership, and thrive in high-pressure environments. My unique blend of clinical expertise and executive coaching makes this program unlike anything else on the market. I bring the depth of resilience training, the rigor of leadership strategy, and the empathy of someone who has walked alongside leaders in moments of triumph and challenge alike.

Program Power Parts:

- Your accelerated program will start within 24 hrs. after purchase
- 1:1 Foundation Call with Coach: Opening session
- A series of assessment screeners
- 3 live virtual 1:1 coaching sessions
- Unlimited private messaging & on-demand messaging support during daily office hours. Plus, 3 floating video office hours per week.
- Copy of my bestselling book, "Evolutionary Resilience"

Unlike traditional leadership coaching that drags out over months, this **accelerated model** delivers results in weeks, not years. A program that gets straight to the core of your resilience needs. **Focused, personalized, and sustainable.**

**Visit my website to start your
Accelerated Leadership Program today!**

www.prudencehatchett.org

9 781969 463679